The
Talking Book
of July

The
Talking Book
of July

Poems *by* Rick Alley

EWU
EASTERN
WASHINGTON
UNIVERSITY
P • R • E • S • S

Cheney, Washington 1997

Library of Congress Cataloging-in-Publication Data

Alley, Rick, 1963-

The talking book of July : poems / by Rick Alley

p.   cm.

ISBN 0-910055-34-3 (alk. paper) ISBN 0-910055-35-1 (pbk. : alk. paper).

I. Title.

PS3551.l448T35 1997

811' .54 — dc21   97-19394
            CIP

Thanks to the editors of the following journals in which these poems first appeared:

Allegheny Review: "Influenza, 1918."
Atom Mind: "The Pond Gets Less Lonely."
Brave Mannequin: "Some Unattainable Facts."
Caliban: "In Spring Air," "There's the Story of the Girl"
    (published as "Folklore"), "I Knew the Dove I Saw on the
    Roof" (published as "On the Way").
College English: "Airfield," "The Man Who Hugs the
    Ground," "The Mayor of Harmony," "The Museum of
    Contemporary Envy."
Conduit: "On Seeing a Friend from a Flattering Distance,"
    "Dissecting Uncle Sorrow."
Hayden's Ferry Review: "Primary Detail."
Poetry East: "Bewildered Again on the Same Street."
Snake Nation Review: "Taking Leave."
Rowboat: "The Radiator."
Willow Springs: "Exemplary Life Above Ground,"
    "With Gratitude, in Depth & Sweet," "Cleaning."

Thanks also to Bill and Betsy Billiter, Frank Johnson,
Peggy Shumaker, Dara Wier, William Corbett,
Nance Van Winckel, Beth Oakes, and James Tate for their
support and good advice.

CONTENTS

for my family,
for Lesley Dauer,
and for Ben Bessent

The
Talking Book
of July

CLEANING

The yard, littered
with dimpled pears, could drowse

for the rest of the day.
White in a field, a claw-footed tub

is reborn as a trough for the cows.
Spent a moment picking up

a perfect ash; it crumbled,
a storm between fingers.

Just now, my hands
in the blue dishwater, I heard

the house settle, complaining old wood.
For a second, the smell of a just-cut field

is a friend who died as a girl.
Easily lost, the mowers call

to each other, waving their shirts.
I'd forgotten voices could travel so far,

that they lose so little on the way.

EXEMPLARY LIFE ABOVE GROUND

For minutes I've done nothing
but watch it
doing nothing,
the marigold bent
with the weight of its bloom.
A true accomplice,
chained to a stem.
Then the newborn
in the house next door
shuts her mouth so the street noise
takes over for a while —
just when I was thinking
I'd like to hear
something befitting the scene.
The marigold swells,
all pollen and blush,
as if daylight placed a bee sting
on its fat, pop-gun head.
Suddenly I favor the edgy clouds,
what the house shadow does
for a peach tree's looks.
Who am I to be so at home
where nothing means so much?
The neighbor's pool is perfectly still,
convinced it's the sky's apprentice.

THE STORM, LEAVING

things on the ground, has become
a cloud behind mountains.
Kicking leaves
and the weak limbs, I am up
and half asleep.
Dizzy spring, loud with flies,
I sense this once a day:
fast blood in the peeling tree,
in the clover,
new and crushed. I can't see
its embarrassing wealth,
but the honeysuckle's there.
From a distance, sometimes people look
like people I know who are gone.

THE MUSEUM OF CONTEMPORARY ENVY

The gulls spiral like cartoon planes,
    their underwater voices
tiny above the earth.

What goes wrong
    goes wrong
wonderfully. Lightning in the pines,

the split of a melon,
    day old kittens
in a desktop drawer

forgotten in the corner of the barn.
    Days exhibit like something to have
which cannot be had

in a blemished world.
    The horses stamp
like kings in their stalls,

the bean field in view,
    the gate open.

WITH GRATITUDE, IN-DEPTH & SWEET

Growing tired of the cabbages
blind in their rows,
growing tired

of lawn deco for Jesus,
I'm going to sit

and watch bats break away
from the shadows of oaks

all night. There's a yellow kitchen
in a neighboring house
I can see from the porch swing

at dusk. A man pauses over
his full sink
with a foaming bouquet of spoons.

They are not sad, the diving bats,
loose in their wrinkled gowns.

I remember a sky
wrapped so tight
the stars were rips, showing through.

THE MAYOR OF HARMONY

To be a ridiculous man
in the failing ridiculous light
requires faith like the water bug
skidding perfectly toward the trout.

I should know.
Sometimes my heart clutches up,
the segmented innards of a fern.

Spreading out, a smashed medallion,
the sun gets fat as it sinks.
Above my window the beat and thump
of raincrows bathing in the gutter.
Look, he said, I'm lucky with a view.

A swanboat bobs alone on the lake.
The lake sizzles with dragonflies.

To be a ridiculous man
in the failing ridiculous light. . . .

The dragonflies glint, poised as darts,
their wings showy as foil.
I'll remember the swan.

When the bird began its dying
it swam deeper into the reeds.

CHOIR BOY

The child happened first
and then my dad,
then the woman who died of her heart.
When the candles drip, I catch the wax,
pure white, drying hard on my hand.
I tell myself I am grown now.
Look, my shadow gets big.
But today on the ice
in my new hat
I covered my mouth when I fell.
Without their leaves, a family of oaks
stands, unused to the view.
I put my hand on the cooling stove.
The heat's like touching a pony.
It's like that dream: a hot light,
my rosary turned into sawdust.
Or the rabbit I found, bleeding
in the snow, and later
on the coat beneath the stairs.
I wasn't sure when I let it go
it would ever run again.

EGGSAC

It was like a cotton raindrop,
the eggsac I found in a pile of grapes
as the colander yawned in the sink.
I forgot about the day,
the sun wrapping my skin like skin,
even the grapes, sweaty and pestered by hornets.
On the cactus, where I hung it,
it glowered, deadpan,
as if breathing "What next?"
I thought about the eggsac,
its parachute cargo,
and wondered myself "What next?"
All night I slept, woke, and slept.
Next morning I slipped it
into a rose dying outside.

What summer hums to the stuffed eggsac!
Sleep, little bleached hands.
Soon you'll endure your first day.

PASSENGER

There's no accounting
for the cherry tree's hue,
that unruly, blossoming wig.
Believe me, I've tried
all the angles, and keep
coming up with a tree
in snow, on a freak spring day,
and everyone squinting his eyes

trying to read
a crooked branch
which writes a sentence
on the sky.

Once, from a car,
I saw a tree
indifferently thumbing dawn.
In a darkened room
with the blinds shut
I saw it again
just now.

An assembly of birds
bedevils a man
made of stone in the park's
dry fountain.
At the foot of a bench
there's a scrap of snow
a nurse mistakes

for a dove. Given the choice
she'd mistake the snow
for a sad, vanishing scarf.

Hours before the bluebird's alarm
I woke in the back of a car.
My friend at the wheel
made a game of the lines
on the road speeding beneath us.
Enraptured, he practiced
his mad slalom
while I drifted, sleepy
and fogged.
I fully believe
we'd have missed dawn
if a branch hadn't pointed it out.

From which corner
of the pond's bilge
did the minnows get their sheen?
Will the children bombing
the water with rocks
doze in the flimsy grass?
From where I stand
the minnows are only
flecks disturbing the glare.
A closer look
and they're quick needles
stitching a tree's reflection.

I KNEW THE DOVE I SAW
ON THE ROOF

couldn't swallow its voice for long.
Sometimes I needed
to be quiet and tired.
From a bus, I watched a colt.
And once, the lip
of a ruined well
gave in to a purple vine.

Entire days, upended and vague,
were stamped on a bus ticket.
Even the dove in its drizzled vest
came to mind now and then
and stayed.

Tall birds with backward knees
pecked at minnows, then flew.
I was the pale stalk
in a bank of ferns
visited once during thunder.

A road that took me places
reminded me of the world.
When I finally arrived in your town,
it was like a map, but real.

ON SEEING A FRIEND
FROM A FLATTERING DISTANCE

Houses played their part,
their insides lit like tiki lamps
blinking in code all night.
Around my heels, the pumpkin field gave
its hairnet of fog to the moon.
The perfect evening, an ugly paradise
godsent, but an unsubtle god.
When I turned around, and saw him
from a distance
at his window like a doll against a screen. . .
Okay, I thought, I'll give that much.
For this one second, I believe.

IN SPRING AIR,

a moth survives
five methods of flight.
The man who thinks
his life hangs from a thread
hasn't been frightened
for days. But I think the cat
laps too loud
and the milk speckles the floor.

Windows jammed for years
are just windows jammed for years.
There is nothing strange
in the mail's delay
or berries in a chipped cup.

I sit in a chair
where the sun hits the lawn,
the sprinkler just missing my knees.
In another place, a white owl
closes its eyes when it kills.

I don't even want to leave
I'm so in love with owls and flight.
I watch my friends
walk around each night
and they haven't been here for years.

THE LAKE OUTSIDE HER WINDOW

does its job.
Swallowing leaves, a child's
red boot. When you record the story,
she says, please remember
the sky heaving its chest.
But will you notice
her wet dress, the various ways
she's not here?

THE POND GETS LESS LONELY

each day. A horse rehearses
how a horse works
on the wet, vanishing hill.
Slick and confused,
the tadpoles scramble,
their flippers resembling legs.
A second later and nothing has changed,
but the horse gets small as it runs.
As a boy I was given an orange to hold
by someone who never came back.
The Jesus frogs were given their name
because they run across water.
I've never been told how Jesus was named
but I remember his hands from a book.
I waited, then walked home to my house,
leaving the orange alone.

AT LAST THE SUN

The man tugging that maple's branch,
how he's showered by wet leaves.
At last the sun, tired worn coin,
cuts a slot in the frothy sky.
He lifts his cane to hook the branch,
pulling with all his life.
I think the town behind his eyes
has gone to sleep, fitfully, in the rain.

THE TALKING BOOK OF JULY

1.
Fern closing like an infant fist,
I've slept too long
beneath open windows,
your fragrance slipping in,
unappeasing,
a thirst for sand.
Now I've fallen out of love
with the unknown,
the print of Jesus
with his feet exposed,
the rock the teacher said
fell from space.
One by one the pears fall
thumping like the dead
at their grass ceiling.
What I want is like the snapshot
of a running man
not in motion
but caught, ready to go.

2.

For hours rain pasted
things against my window:
river-veined oak leaves
with the grasp of lizards,
a moth, lightly speckled
with powder for wings.
When the sun came back
I hardly recognized the view.
The young goat, lost all day,
follows the bell at her neck.
Soon they'll comb the woods
in their muddy, pop-eyed trucks
yelling for the goat
like children,
the inventors of that much faith.

3.
Occasionally a woodthrush
scared up above the treeline
and music from nearby squatters,
clapping like cymbals of air.
Having not spoken
to a soul for three days
(except in the dreamy city
I populate in sleep)
I've forgotten my voice, a book
one is never sure of reading.
Sometimes I think of the goat
nibbling alone in her travels.
When the bell's rattle
trickles by on a breeze,
I sip the air like I'm swimming,
as if anything might happen.

SNAPSHOT

A moth escaping a rose's lips
looks like a bed sheet
stolen by wind. *Sunday Evening, 1964,*
my father's watch
an ugly glint. For all those years
stuffed in a purse, discarded
in a jammed-shut drawer. . . .
the crumpled photo, slick as an eye
staring back at me,
the snoop. When the man on the bus
pointed out a grove
of lemon trees slicing the mist,
for a second his breath
bloomed on the window. I could almost
make out the grove.

INFLUENZA, 1918

This morning, a yellowjacket drilled itself
through a hole in my window screen.
Noon, the men who collect the dead
came tapping at the drawing room window.
They cupped paper masks over their mouths.
I waved them on. No one today.

Last week it was baby G.
A sign went up on the front porch
and we were told to keep doors shut,
windows down. Mother and I watched
as they wrapped my sister in canvas.
Later, the cart that took her away
passed with many clumsy parcels.

Whenever I enter mother's room
she screams *get out,* fever rising from her bed
in a burnt spice. I've timed the patrol men
and know when it's safe to lift my window,
rest my chin on the ledge
and taste the September frost. This morning
a yellowjacket, alone and out of season,

brought light into my room. If this is a sign,
let it be urgent and true.

MORNING IS BUSY

rebuilding itself. I like moss
holding on to walls;
it is stubborn, patiently green.
A cloud on roots, the white tree
hurts so I close my eyes.

Bathers walking away from the shore
go to where they are going.
We shiver, dressed in our wet skin
underneath the mild sky.

It's easy to think where we live
will always be beginning.
No one goes near the bent reeds
or the loose, damaged pier.

The body found last season
has never been so gone.
I can cover my face with one hand
and still see the blossoms.

SPRING WAS PLANNING A
QUIET COMEBACK

There were times my heart
was a kerchief in a pocket,
suddenly producing a dove.
Muffled by a coat in a closet upstairs
an alarm clock went off its head.
Spring was planning a quiet comeback,
kissing the elms
with a train wreck of buds.
I thought of childhood as a child
taking notes on a frosted window.
"I was here," which was nowhere at all
to the bulbs digging their flowerbed graves.
Sometimes a clock was a heart
in a coat, a tree
was a jailbreak of leaves.
I climbed to the top
till the neighborhood looked
easy to take and take in.

AIRFIELD

On my porch in a late April,
early evening orange with dusk,
I watch a plane take off
from the field across the street
and the boys who mimic the plane,
running through their yards
with arms for wings.
    When the bee hits
the inner basin of my ear
I think all the rumblings
of the engine-filled world
have come to play a concert in my head.
    Once, by a river,
after the sting of a wasp,
I watched a friend pack mud
on his swollen hand
then stumble home like a puppet.
When the pain doesn't come
    I swat the bee away.
It hovers, an earring beside my hair.
Houses fade into hills beyond the field,
diminished by evening, orange with dusk.
    A plane starts up
in the field's far corner.
It purrs like sun on wet grass.

UP EARLY AND OUT

in plum-colored dawn,
she thinks she was born
arranging a tear.
The pliers she'll use to clip the rose
were left out overnight
and are wet. One look
at the spider's minaret,
at the mat drying on the porch.
Does the ivy want
to flourish on the gate,
making a deadbolt of leaves?
Every night the same dream:
disassembling a berry, an ant.
She thinks of the rose of Jericho,
dead, but protecting good seed.

FOUR POEMS INSTEAD
OF AN ELEGY

1.
The dogwoods, fully open
and dripping in the sun.
Your mother, driving with the windows down,
practicing life without you.
Already the hospice is trying to call.
She'll find she's rehearsed it all wrong.

2.
Years later, I'm walking with a friend.
Above us, a jet
makes a slow line.
I remember my friend is leaving next day.
We walk on, beneath the jet stream's trail.

3.
Of the dogwoods I ask one thing:
to be left alone
with this green June,
its wet, buzzing days.
With every intention of seeing your grave
I drove to the country,
caught up in the view.
There are flowers so apt at being themselves
a glance takes time, is expensive.

4.
Violet, chrysanthemum, bougainvillea's bruised light.
In my closet, your shirt hangs perfect, exact.
A homing bee, hooked on a breeze,
skirts a paper lantern.
The dogwoods, brilliant in the dry sun,
are almost too white to be seen.

THE MAN FROM BALTIMORE

Only the hedges heard the sky rustle.
Leaves went browsing
like windblown pilgrims.
The suitcase, abandoned by the infinite roadside,
lay empty and smelled of guitars.
Boondy launched it into the filmy pond.
We laughed when it bubbled and sank.
The man from Baltimore moved in that day
with his pottery and two coats.
The wax mustache appeared soon after.
The dramatic Thursdays, his boots beneath a bridge.
The sky was dingy, plums in milk,
and the daffodils stared at the ground.
By turns we spied through the dusty hedge
on the man bathing in the lake.
He looked like some wet vegetable,
pink and clinging to its last bit of earth.

ROCK GARDEN

Even this one seems to bloom,
quarry-gray but pretty.
Perhaps it was hurled
through a florist's window
and rolled out smelling
sweet. Still, there's something
of the mud-flow about it,
an ugly, gravel-pit charm.
Just think of the farmer
who broke his spade, the kid
who tripped, skinning her knee.
The years gone to waste
by the compost pile
somehow resulting
in this: an attractive display
of similar stones,
a bench and a stringy pine.
All the time in the world
to mull it over. Even secret lives
have secret lives.

THE MAN WHO HUGS
THE GROUND

presses his face
close to a puddle. He would take me
for his own reflection, a floating
clump of wool. So I tell him
he's needed as the sky's
blue wash. That men have
built bridges. Women
rivet the seams
of the earth. When he laughs
a tuft of air
disturbs the brown water. Listen,
I say. Once I tried praying
without mentioning names.
My own botched it up.
I tell him lovers subtract
into pools of linen. Flowers
drop their own. That a puddle
is not so rare. One is always
on the make. For a moment
the mud is kind to his face
then sinks it completely under.

THE BEST AND FINAL CHAPTER

In the best and final chapter
a boy sleeps beneath his bed.
I was reading, getting sleepy,
in the laundromat's
hot glare.
first thunder, then a siren,
then a draft
disturbing the page.
Whoever walked in
let the door close slow
like it had to make up
its own mind.
I didn't see the cars collide.
I looked up when I heard the smash.
Beyond my chair
and the spotty door
a city shook out
its bedclothes. The drivers bickered,
nervy but safe,
so this was not a terrible place.
I was glad the boy had fallen asleep.
It was good for a sequel. It was good.

BEWILDERED AGAIN ON
THE SAME STREET,

I saw lilacs, ducks, a fat black bee.
Today the sky could be a wave
seen from an ocean's floor. I go on being more
than one thing. Like always, I'm at least two.
You thought we were reading in the next room
when we were listening to you cry,
breathless. The tightrope walker gathered herself
and casually stepped between buildings.
We see her expression on faces we know,
our little but dangerous faith.
When a friend dies, you call other friends.
I told you, I can be more.
The sparrow with dirt in the fold of its wing
was glad to remember the ground.

FIELD GUIDE TO AUTUMN

As if something it said
startled the breeze, the breeze
snaps back at a maple. Days are restless,
a few blank sparrows
noisy with nothing to say.
Should you arrive
on a see-for-yourself tour
please notice there are rules.
The pond asks a considerable toll
and then you're on your own.

Where the bulldozer left
    a bite in the field
I found a scribbling freeway
    of tadpoles. Enough to dazzle
an unnamed cat
    into touching its face in water.
Today I endured
    the unbearable din
of a butterfly tasting a salt lick.
    It was good when a plane
swept sparrows from the pines.
    As I write, clouds dismantle.

Spent the morning
clearing brambles. A gate needed a latch.
There's a building's foundation
beneath bedsprings and vines.
Often, someone on a distant path
will wave without any incentive.

ONE-ACT

October's become a permanent fixture,
a jaunty new mood for the lawn.
The neighbor's kid, as the dying villain,
stabs the fresh leaf-fall with a stick.
Applause of sparrows in the chestnuts
as the sun, blushing, lowers
for good.

(At night, man
leaning his forehead
on a window
looks like an old moon
through a sheet of ice.)

SOME UNATTAINABLE FACTS

After several days
they reached a decision:
the little blue apples
collecting frost on their tops
were lovely and not to be knocked down.
When a gust ripped one of the finest,
leaving only the stem on the tree
and the apple a deep bruise in the grass,
a meeting was held.
The apples were clipped and sealed
in a barrel of peat.
Paris loved Josephine Baker.
America did not.
The herring merchant rolled the parcel
into the sea
and the apples landed in France.
France is a lovely country,
brimming like a glass of juice
in the lap of a sleeping child.

CURRENT EVENTS

In the rain's beaded curtain,
its broken spill,
there's the noise of a morning
rushing toward noon. I hear it
through doors, in the patter of leaves
slick above neighboring roofs.
    Sometimes when I'm walking
the breadth of this house,
its effects seem vague, noncommittal:
dust is a lamp shade's
dingy rain, the skylight's the belly
of a glass-bottom boat, wrecked
with a slip of cloud.
    A ball of paper shifts on the desk
the way books crammed
on a tight shelf
breathe when one is removed.
And I thought I was alone in the house
with this rain, an off-screen kiss.

PRIMARY DETAIL

I didn't know why he was falling.
From his hill, I'd decided
he could see the beach.
It would be small, without grace.
A few birds dotting the sand.
Maybe a ship, misty from distance.
What puzzled me most
was the hill itself. How it figured in
with the scene. At one point
he was slipping with the sand,
deliberate, a calculated fall.
All the way to the level beach
and where the beach became wet.
I even had him scooping
handfuls of sand.
Picking out the tiny crabs.
But there was nowhere
for him to go. On his hill again
the wind sounded like boys
shaking apples from a tree. This time
he jumped. For real. Thinking about
his most serious loves. Taking
them all with him.

THE ORPHANS

Our mother is buried across the river.
Look what we go through to visit her.
An arrow of birds parts a hedge
and we duck beneath the orange leaves.
Bobolinks huddle in a bowl of moss.
Look what we go through
to catch them. At night, picking nettles
from the elbows of our coats,
we swap twigs with a match
and get fire. As midnight constructs
a blanket of holes
we're curled in dirt, dragonfly nymphs.
When we sleep, we cross our arms
so the stars might think
they're reflected in a distant, black pool.

RAINY LAKE

Bronze-plate, dividing into wings,
the beetle clamped tight in my hair.
It held when my sister
pinched it out,
getting louder before letting go.

A breeze kicks up
summer's dusty skirts.
Junebugs click against the window.
The rose I've watched going brown all month
leans its head against my house.
Like paper around a firecracker
its petals curl into ash.
Of all the ways to chart a flower's withering,
all the names to name its sweet rot,
my sister shakes aphids
into a bowl of turpentine.
I sniff the air,
watching the insects forget how to swim.

In the dark,
the TV blinks white, then blue.
A door slams, a shutting book.
You used to say that to leave this world
one must first make a world
of the body.

In order to pay her respects to fear
my sister lit the shed on fire.
The roses bowed into the smoky blaze,
drying up like pods
turning black for autumn.
Christ, in his denial, made desire
more attractive.
The floorboards sank into a charred bowl
as the possum escaped with her young.

fifty-two million years away from Mars,
I scan the bedroom window for planets.
Night wears on, thinning,
the ruins of a veil.
In the picture you painted of the rainy lake
there are trees that could be people
imitating trees.
In the night that imitates itself each night
the rose lessens, becoming finished.

THEY ARE ALWAYS TRYING

to go away,
the flowers that break
in the wind. Returning yellow
to the same earth,
they're alive twice in the world.
Seeds drop from the maple in spring,
spiraling down through leaves.
I've seen grass growing on roofs
and a fish etched in stone.
My body always runs low —
half a degree, since birth.
There's a bug so cold
it would quickly die
in the warmth of a human hand.

AT HOME IN A LASTING BODY

Tonight a cricket, fat as a knot,
      closes up into a breathing hinge.
I can hear a siren

miles away, sounding tiny as a thimble of fire.
      For however long its evening lasts
the cricket rehearses a brittle complaint:

always less than a lilac's shadow,
      always the grackle, tripping on leaves.
I imagine the lilacs above the drive

as snow falling off bells.
      Still, the cricket insists that summer
is here and a root-bellied friend.

For however long the siren lasts
      it shrinks till it's not a siren.
The cricket, at home in a lasting body,

gives anchor to a flowering weed.

VIRGINIA WOOLF,

vans pass, loaded with kids
aimed at the boardwalk's arcade.
Saw a pelican fly
with its scoop of a mouth,
heavy above the dunes.
Thunder whips the clouds to sheets,
but the storm holds back,
never shows.
Last night I saw the water blink
beneath lightning, quick and thin.
Today I walk through gravel and shells
to the strip where town begins.
Virginia, they're selling hermit crabs
in wire cages as pets.
The same birds run from the tide —
the ones that ran while you sat.
All day, the ocean sounds like a storm
contained in an empty barrel.
I thought I saw you tucked in a wave.
You looked like a windy dress.

I DON'T THINK THE NEW GEARS

of morning will ever stop.
A mayfly, deep
in its hour life,
braves a daisy's stem.
Twice, I thought
a jarring truck
on the street was early thunder.
I wanted May
broken and done
but keep finding ways
it succeeds. The asphalt's bright
and burns my eyes.
Dew would dissolve the fly.
Last night, the rabbit
I found on the curb
looked like it was running
asleep. A man props
a silver ladder
against a tree, breathing.
I'll be finishing up
my slow walk home
just as he reaches the top.

HER FEATURELESS DAY

folds up on itself.
The cows are positioned
just so.
She lifts the lids
off dinner's full boil
and the windows cloud
like sleep.

How she loves to wrap the batter
into a death mask of her thumb!
The windows begin to sweat.
The sun slips into
a pocket of brine.
The calf quickens in the belly.

DISSECTING UNCLE SORROW

His night job is insomnia.
He seals pacts with a wink.
In all the lit buildings
of all the lit towns
he's got pillow-punching down
to a faith. His songbook includes
"I'll Be Happy, Soon"
and "The Amazing
Night-Blooming Tear."
At dawn, he's the woman
with the strong, small hand
holding her robe closed.
"What else do you want?"
I scream at her face
and the hand tightens its grip.
If that's not enough
he's the tepid coffee
I drink and return to next day.
He's the guard in the park
walking alone
and he can walk a very long way.

THERE'S THE STORY OF THE GIRL

caught in the rafters
and the granary, standing in fog.

A moment balanced on the quick spine
of a robin observing a plum.

I am always lost, going back;
my house is not my hat.

Her parents would be a lake
and a town. I found the road

I was looking for,
the one going past the barn.

When the time came, the girl was afraid
to let go of the beam and climb down.

The spider she saw was combing its web.
The hay was bright and changed.

A bird flew by, at home in a world
where landing is easy and safe.

THE CANARY MAN & YOU

He hunched a broomstick
behind his neck,
balanced his cages
and left town.
A riot of mosquitoes
paraded him away.
You sucked ice slivers
on the Methodist's porch,
watching evening slide
into a black lake.
Your hand, cold from the ice,
slipped into your pants
like someone else.
The whole town buckled.

A blue hound was nibbling
on a plate of grass
when it found the stiff yellow clumps
which it brought, one by one,
to your feet.
Summer withered by the mossy bog,
his hand an empty space in yours.

FOR MARY JANE, OPEN AND
LOOKING FORWARD

The bush beneath my window
grows into shadow,
into a bulk of night
shrugging its shoulders.
Wind clicks the lattice
on the broken patio gate.
It whistles like you
waiting outside.
Pretending I was blind,
you'd steer me around the yard,
not with my eyes closed
but open and looking forward.
At the end of August,
stuffed in my small man's suit,
I sat through your funeral
swollen and allergic
to the sweet yellow flowers.
I remember the card
you bragged over at the bus stop,
LION'S CLUB and DONOR
stamped above your name.
For weeks I suspected anyone
who looked into my eyes.

THE RADIATOR

leaked a river beside my bed.
Steam spouted up
a few ghostly canoes.
Goodbye grandpa, your fists dripping empty.
I'll see you in that photo, holding melons.
The radiator got too hot
and I slept outside.
The radiator was cracked and stained the floor.
When I woke up it had hissed away
my third complicated affair.
The radiator came home one night,
drunk, and stayed forever.
It crouched against the wall, a smoky accordion.
I became the giant, the crook, the damp
leprous angel.
The evening was contagious.
The radiator gargled dimes.
The world outside the window
shimmied with all the wind in the world.

MY SHOES DISAPPEAR

in the grass.
In shifting light
the field takes on
the sheen of a changing lake.
A bleached fence
sewn with vines
is caught trying to lie down.
No one's in the clearing
where I want to be,
no one to mend the shed.
I've thought of the grave
hidden in weeds
I found while chasing a ball.
The ugly stone stood unamazed.
Days will be lit
in profusion.
The charming heads
of the wild burrs
are hooked and hurt when they catch.
The locust, clipped
to a dry branch,
could easily belong to the tree.

THE IDENTITIES OF THE DEAD

I thought they'd go away
like the bodies they were glued to.
Clumsy, I wanted to lose them all
through a hole in a silk pocket.
A child attends
another child's wake
and is stunned by an aunt's dark glove.
I thought it wise to gulp them down
in one easy swallow.
Not me, I said. Take it somewhere else,
the glimmer of your tell-all lips.
I thought they'd go away.
Made plans. Invented endings
where the wounded stand up, unharmed.

GROUND

1.

Someone in white beneath the hedges
in the blue night.
Locusts sizzle and click.
The house sleeps as if it's deep water
or a fist of moss, growing in a well.
When I squeeze my eyes shut, the body on the lawn
becomes a naked fish
then a pool of silver. I open them again
and the whole world moves.

2.

Not these maples, swollen with rain.
Or that girl, packing a rope
into a basket.
Not the bobwhites.
They interrupt each other
with their names.
The girl will go, permanent and finished.
The birds, machinery in the trees.
But because I have fallen asleep on the lawn
I wake thinking of the dead.
I refuse to make them lovely, memory's drapes.
My friend who died alone, her story
begins in the middle.
Snow had covered the lawn.
There was simply nowhere to go.

3.
In the long grass, crows loot a goat.
The goat is dead,
two jelled coins for eyes in its head.
I watch you whip the air
with a stick.
The crows scatter like buckshot.

Did I say summer began on the lawn?
This morning
I watched three hornets
sipping a pear's soft wound.

4. (PICNIC)
For a while I fingered the seams
of the little barnyard
on your shirt.
When the child came screaming
toward us
we noticed the fly, the delicate skull
of the egg.

5.
Something gives my room
the look of a place that is ending,
a city you can walk to
but is always far away.
Maybe I'm just in bed, sleeping.
If so, I'd wake and lose this morning
somewhere in the day.
I'd like something amazing to happen:
a column of ants
coming down my wall, carrying
a child's glove.

THE GROWING DAYS

were becoming less sane.
We stayed clear
of the wasp's nest.
When it rained, we watched
from behind a screen
on a porch, getting wet.
My thin aunt was sick at night.
We could hear her smooth gown.
We knew we'd all change someday;
sometimes, we compared our hands.
The growing days grew without us
till some of us left, waving.
With paper hips, the wasp flew close
to our eyes, our moving hands.

TAKING LEAVE

I'd like to live in the blue coat,
the one forgotten in the park.

Will winter always begin like this,
a life sentence

in a cup of tea?
The wind chimes move, but not enough

to cause much of a stir.
I thought I heard the brittle gears

of a network of ice in the trees.
High up, the sun

chooses what to touch —
last night's frost, the wind chime's throat.

I'd like to follow the black birds
that stamp their marks into the snow.

Are the children standing in the new snow
praying or looking at a child?

Because the birds will go away, I can think
of the birds as gone.

THE ROBINS DIM, COMING BACK
A LITTLE LESS

Young willows line the street.
All the lengthy, well-designed days.

I go on with my walk
then stoop to pick up
a stone, smooth as a thumb.

Once I believed a stone thrown clear
through a window resulted in . . .

Now the willows are shattered by light
that touches the edges of leaves.

One day the season will splinter and end.

I think a god must be small
and very quiet
to covet the bloodworm, writhing.

BED POEM

One day the season will splinter and end.
Who on earth will mend it?

Dawn took all day
to get out of my head;
now, nearly midnight, it's back.

When I woke, my fist
was a rose made of dough
slowly unfolding

beside me. Hummingbirds stalled
in the busy oleander

catching their breath
between sips.

Like sleep stripping a face blank,
midnight fogs and darkens.

Sometimes it seems the world has grown.
Sometimes it grows very small.

Born in 1963 in Kingsport, Tennessee, Rick Alley spent most of his years growing up in Virginia Beach, Virginia. He was educated at Old Dominion University and later received his M.F.A. in poetry from the University of Massachusetts — Amherst. He has worked both as an editorial assistant for the Associated Writing Programs and as editor of *Marquee*, a journal of poetry and one-act plays. Currently, he lives in Norfolk, Virginia where he teaches literature and creative writing as well as working with a correspondence writing program for teenagers through Johns Hopkins University. He has recently completed work on his second book of poems.